That's Life

Day-to-Day Stories and Language Activities

HIGH BEGINNING

Ann Gianola

Instructor, San Diego Community College District
Instructor, University of San Diego English Language Academy
San Diego, California

New Readers Press

That's Life: Day-to-Day Stories and Language Activities
High-Beginning Level
ISBN 978-1-56420-780-7

Copyright © 2008 New Readers Press
New Readers Press
ProLiteracy's Publishing Division
101 Wyoming Street, Syracuse, New York 13204
www.newreaderspress.com

Printed in the United States of America
12 11 10

Proceeds from the sale of New Readers Press materials support professional
development, training, and technical assistance programs of ProLiteracy
that benefit local literacy programs in the U.S. and around the globe.

Developmental Editor: Karen Davy
Creative Director: Andrea Woodbury
Illustrations: James P. Wallace
Production Specialist: Maryellen Casey

Contents

Lesson 1

The Same Routine

The radio wakes Bruno up every morning. This morning, there is a commercial on the radio. *"Is your life the same day after day? Are you tired of the same routine? Visit Mexico!"* Bruno opens his eyes and listens. It's true. Every morning is the same routine. Bruno gets up and eats cereal and milk for breakfast. He takes a shower, shaves, brushes his teeth, and gets dressed. Then he takes the number 7 bus downtown. The bus isn't crowded, so Bruno sits in the front.

Bruno doesn't want his life to be the same day after day. He thinks he needs to change his routine. Bruno can't go to Mexico, but his life can be more exciting. Today Bruno eats some leftover pizza for breakfast. He shaves before he takes a shower. He gets dressed before he brushes his teeth. Bruno takes the number 9 bus downtown.

The number 9 bus is crowded. Bruno has to stand in the back. His stomach hurts. Leftover pizza is not a very good breakfast. His face hurts, too. It's better to shave after you take a shower. Then Bruno sees some toothpaste on his shirt. It's better to get dressed after you brush your teeth. "My routine is fine," thinks Bruno. "But maybe I need a new radio station."

Answer the questions.

1. What wakes Bruno up every morning?

2. What does Bruno do after he gets up?

3. Which bus does he take downtown? Where does he sit?

4. What does Bruno think he needs to change?

5. What does Bruno eat for breakfast today?

6. When does he shave and get dressed?

7. Which bus does he take downtown?

8. Where does he have to stand?

9. When is it better to shave?

10. What does Bruno see on his shirt?

Complete the sentences.

brushes	hurts	is	takes
shaves	doesn't want	thinks	eats

1. Bruno _____ his life to be the same day after day.

2. Today Bruno _____ some leftover pizza for breakfast.

3. He _____ before he takes a shower.

4. He gets dressed before he _____ his teeth.

5. Bruno _____ the number 9 bus downtown.

6. The bus _____ crowded. Bruno has to stand in the back.

7. His stomach _____. His face hurts, too.

8. "My routine is fine," _____ Bruno.

Matching: Definitions

_____ 1. commercial   a. what you use to clean your teeth

_____ 2. pizza   b. an electronic device that transmits voices and music

_____ 3. toothpaste   c. round bread with tomato sauce and cheese

_____ 4. routine   d. an advertisement on the radio or TV

_____ 5. radio   e. the internal body part where food goes

_____ 6. stomach   f. the things you do regularly

Talking to a Co-Worker

Practice the dialog with a partner.

A. You have something on your shirt.

B. Yes, I see it. I'll wash it off in the restroom.

A. What is it?

B. It's toothpaste. This morning, I got dressed before I brushed my teeth.

A. It's better to get dressed after you brush your teeth.

B. Oh, I know. But I needed to change my routine.

A Change in the Routine

What does Bruno think after he changes his routine? Read the example. Then write new sentences starting with *It's better to.*

New Routine	**Later, Bruno thinks:**
1. Bruno eats some leftover pizza for breakfast.	It's better to eat cereal and milk.
2. He shaves before he takes a shower.	
3. He gets dressed before he brushes his teeth.	
4. He takes the number 9 bus downtown.	
5. Bruno listens to the same radio station.	

Listening

Listen. Check (✔) the correct sentence.

1. ____ a. There is music.
   ____ b. There is an advertisement.

2. ____ a. Bruno does the same things.
   ____ b. Bruno does different things.

3. ____ a. He can go to Mexico.
   ____ b. His life can be more exciting.

4. ____ a. Bruno sits in the front.
   ____ b. Bruno has to stand in the back.

5. ____ a. His stomach hurts.
   ____ b. His face hurts.

6. ____ a. His face hurts.
   ____ b. His feet hurt.

7. ____ a. There is toothpaste on his shirt.
   ____ b. There is pizza on his shirt.

8. ____ a. He needs a new routine.
   ____ b. He needs a new radio station.

Pronunciation and Writing

Say the words from the story. Write the number of syllables in each word. Underline the stressed syllable.

1. <u>toothpaste</u> _2_

2. exciting ____

3. routine ____

4. leftover ____

5. crowded ____

6. station ____

7. stomach ____

8. commercial ____

9. downtown ____

10. brushes ____

11. cereal ____

12. breakfast ____

13. shower ____

14. pizza ____

15. radio ____

What about you?

Circle *Yes* or *No.* Then write questions and ask your partner.

Yes No 1. I have the same routine every morning.

<u>Do you have the same routine every morning?</u>

Yes No 2. I need to change my routine.

_____

Yes No 3. I sometimes eat cereal and milk for breakfast.

_____

Yes No 4. I sometimes eat leftover pizza for breakfast.

_____

Yes No 5. I get dressed after I brush my teeth.

_____

Topics for Discussion or Writing

1. Do you listen to the radio? If so, what radio station do you usually listen to?

2. Do you take the bus to school or work? If so, what is the bus number? Where do you sit or stand?

3. Do you want your life to be the same day after day? How can your life be more exciting?

Lesson 2

The Anniversary Party

Tonight there is a big celebration for Edward and Sally. It's a party for their 25th wedding anniversary. There is rock music and delicious Chinese food. There are pretty red decorations. It's a beautiful evening outside.

Edward and Sally's children, nieces, nephews, brothers, sisters, and cousins are all there. Their good friends and neighbors also come. Everyone is very happy.

But there is one person who isn't happy. She is Irma, Sally's 82-year-old mother. She is never happy. In her opinion, things aren't quite right. Because the music is rock, Irma says, "Classical is better." Because the food is Chinese, she says, "Mexican is better." Because the decorations are red, she says, "Green is better." Because the party is outside, she says, "Inside is better." Still, Edward and Sally are enjoying their party. They listen to the best wishes of their other guests.

"Happy Anniversary!" says Edward's nephew, Gary.

"Congratulations!" says Sally's sister, Donna.

Irma wants to say something, too. The music stops. Everyone is quiet. "Howard," says Irma. "You are a wonderful man. You are perfect for my daughter." Everyone looks uncomfortable. Then the music starts again.

Sally walks up to her mother. "Mother," she whispers. "You forget. My husband's name is not Howard. It's Edward."

"I know," says Irma. "But Howard is better."

Answer the questions.

1. What are Edward and Sally having a party for?

2. What kind of food is there? What color are the decorations?

3. Who is at the party?

4. Who is Irma? How is she?

5. What does Irma say about the food and decorations?

6. What do Edward and Sally listen to?

7. What does Edward's nephew, Gary, say?

8. What does Sally's sister, Donna, say?

9. What does Irma say when the music stops?

10. How does everyone look?

What is the category?

music	nieces	decorations	"Congratulations!"
"Best wishes!"	food	"Good for you!"	guests
nephews	cousins	brothers	"Happy Anniversary!"

Family Members	Things at a Party	Things to Say at a Party
1. _____	1. _____	1. _____
2. _____	2. _____	2. _____
3. _____	3. _____	3. _____
4. _____	4. _____	4. _____

Matching: Definitions

_____ 1. opinion   a. a date you remember every year

_____ 2. guests   b. things that make a place look more beautiful

_____ 3. celebration   c. people who are visiting your home

_____ 4. anniversary   d. the children of your aunt or uncle

_____ 5. cousins   e. your ideas or beliefs

_____ 6. decorations   f. a party for a special day

Conversation at a Party

Practice the dialog with a partner.

A. Happy Anniversary!

B. Thank you so much. And thanks for coming.

A. I'm really happy to be here.

B. How's your food?

A. It's delicious. Chinese food is my favorite.

B. Good. Eat a lot and enjoy yourself.

Irma's Opinion

What does Irma say about the party? Read the example. Then write new sentences.

The Party	**Irma says:**
1. The music is rock.	_Classical is better._
2. The food is Chinese.	
3. The decorations are red.	
4. The party is outside.	
5. Her daughter's husband is named Edward.	

Listening

Listen. Check (✔) the correct sentence.

1. ____ a. It's their 25th anniversary.
   ____ b. It's Irma's 82nd birthday.

2. ____ a. Their family is there.
   ____ b. Friends and neighbors are there.

3. ____ a. She is Donna, Sally's sister.
   ____ b. She is Irma, Sally's mother.

4. ____ a. She is enjoying the party.
   ____ b. She is never happy.

5. ____ a. Irma likes rock music.
   ____ b. Irma doesn't like rock music.

6. ____ a. "Happy Anniversary!"
   ____ b. "Mexican is better."

7. ____ a. Everyone is quiet.
   ____ b. Everyone looks uncomfortable.

8. ____ a. Irma forgets Edward's name.
   ____ b. Irma doesn't like Edward's name.

Pronunciation and Writing

Say the words from the story. Write the number of syllables in each word. Underline the stressed syllable.

1. beautiful ____

2. uncomfortable ____

3. congratulations ____

4. inside ____

5. delicious ____

6. whispers ____

7. nieces ____

8. anniversary ____

9. classical ____

10. celebration ____

11. wonderful ____

12. quiet ____

13. opinion ____

14. decorations ____

15. outside ____

What about you?

Circle *Yes* or *No.* Then write questions and ask your partner.

Yes   No   1. I sometimes have celebrations.

<u>Do you sometimes have celebrations?</u>

Yes   No   2. I invite family, friends, and neighbors to parties.

_____

Yes   No   3. I like rock music.

_____

Yes   No   4. I like Chinese food.

_____

Yes   No   5. I know someone who is never happy.

_____

Topics for Discussion or Writing

1. Do people have celebrations for 25th wedding anniversaries in your native country? What do they do?

2. What other kinds of celebrations can people have? What are good things to say at those celebrations?

3. Who do you invite when you have a celebration?

Lesson 3

The Traffic Jam

It's 7:45 A.M. Peter is driving his car to work. It's only a ten-minute drive, but sometimes there is traffic at rush hour. Peter turns right on Highland Avenue. Suddenly, Peter needs to slow down. There are a lot of cars. Then he needs to stop completely. Peter can't go straight. Many cars are stopped in front of him. Peter can't turn left or right. He can't make a U-turn. "Oh, no!" says Peter. He is stuck in a terrible traffic jam.

A man on a motorcycle passes Peter's car. "Riding a motorcycle is faster than driving," thinks Peter. A woman on a bicycle passes Peter's car. "Riding a bicycle is faster than driving," thinks Peter. A man jogging on the sidewalk passes Peter's car. "Jogging is faster than driving," thinks Peter. A woman walking her dog on the sidewalk passes Peter's car. Now Peter is angry. He hits the steering wheel. "This is ridiculous!" he shouts. "Walking a dog is faster than driving!"

Finally, the police arrive to help clear the traffic jam. Peter can drive again, but he is thirty minutes late for work. Peter's co-worker, Ramon, asks, "What happened? Did you walk to work?"

"No," said Peter. "But I *will* walk tomorrow. Believe me, it's faster than driving!"

Answer the questions.

1. What is Peter doing at 7:45 A.M.?

2. How long is the drive to work?

3. Which way does Peter turn on Highland Avenue?

4. What is he stuck in?

5. What does a man on a motorcycle do?

6. Who passes Peter's car on a bicycle?

7. What does Peter think about jogging?

8. What is the woman on the sidewalk doing?

9. Who arrives to help clear the traffic jam?

10. How late is Peter for work?

Complete the sentences.

bicycle	steering wheel	traffic jam	rush hour
sidewalk	dog	car	motorcycle

1. Peter is driving his _____ to work.

2. Sometimes there is traffic at _____.

3. He is stuck in a terrible _____.

4. A man on a _____ passes Peter's car.

5. A woman on a _____ passes Peter's car.

6. A man jogging on the _____ passes Peter's car.

7. A woman walking her _____ on the sidewalk passes Peter's car.

8. Peter is angry. He hits the _____.

Match the words and pictures.

go straight	turn right	turn left	make a U-turn

  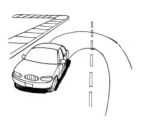 

1. _____ 2. _____ 3. _____ 4. _____

Talking to a Co-Worker

Practice the dialog with a partner.

A. Sorry I'm late.

B. What happened?

A. I was stuck in a terrible traffic jam.

B. Where were you?

A. On Highland Avenue. A woman walking a dog passed me!

B. Well, there's always traffic at rush hour.

Check the good ideas.

You are late for work and stuck in a terrible traffic jam. Check (✔) the things that are good to do. Write other ideas on the lines below.

_____ hit the steering wheel

_____ wait patiently

_____ drive on the sidewalk

_____ relax and listen to music

_____ buy a motorcycle

_____ call work on your cell phone

_____ get out of your car and walk

_____ honk the horn

_____ listen to the police

_____ make a U-turn if it's safe

_____   _____

Listening

Listen. Check (✔) the correct sentence.

1. ____ a. It's 5:45 A.M.

   ____ b. It's 7:45 A.M.

2. ____ a. He needs to stop completely.

   ____ b. He needs to slow down.

3. ____ a. He can't turn left.

   ____ b. He can't go in the same direction.

4. ____ a. He can't turn around.

   ____ b. He can't turn right.

5. ____ a. He drives past Peter's car.

   ____ b. He is stuck behind Peter's car.

6. ____ a. He hits his co-worker.

   ____ b. He hits the steering wheel.

7. ____ a. Peter can drive again.

   ____ b. The police stop Peter.

8. ____ a. Peter is an hour and a half late.

   ____ b. Peter is half an hour late.

Pronunciation and Writing

Say the words from the story. Write the number of syllables in each word. Underline the stressed syllable.

1. traffic ____

2. suddenly ____

3. police ____

4. walking ____

5. terrible ____

6. motorcycle ____

7. driving ____

8. sidewalk ____

9. ridiculous ____

10. angry ____

11. faster ____

12. passes ____

13. completely ____

14. jogging ____

15. bicycle ____

What about you?

Circle *Yes* or *No*. Then write questions and ask your partner.

Yes **No** 1. I go to work at rush hour.

Do you go to work at rush hour? _____

Yes **No** 2. I drive a car to work.

_____

Yes **No** 3. I ride a motorcycle to work.

_____

Yes **No** 4. I ride a bicycle to work.

_____

Yes **No** 5. I sometimes get stuck in a terrible traffic jam.

_____

Topics for Discussion or Writing

1. Where is the traffic very bad in your city?

2. Are you sometimes late for work? If so, why are you late?

3. What do you do when you are angry?

Lesson 4

A Secret Recipe

Sophie is making a chicken and rice casserole. It's for a party tonight at her sister's home. Sophie is looking at the recipe while she is cutting up the ingredients. Sophie stops and takes a drink of her coffee. Then she looks back at her cookbook. She reads, "Add 1½ quarts of chicken stock." Sophie converts that to 48 ounces. That's a lot of liquid! But that's what the recipe says. Sophie measures the stock and pours it into the casserole dish. Now the casserole dish is overflowing. She needs to move everything into a big pot. This chicken and rice casserole looks very strange.

Sophie looks at the recipe again. Sophie is wrong. The recipe doesn't say, "Add 1½ quarts of chicken stock." It says, "Add 1½ *cups* of chicken stock." That's only 12 ounces. Sophie was looking at a recipe for chicken and rice *soup!* Sophie looks into the pot. She stirs it for a while. Actually, it looks and smells really good. Sophie thinks, "Okay, now this is chicken and rice casserole soup."

In the evening, Sophie brings her soup to the party. Everyone likes it. "Your soup is delicious," says her sister. "What is it?"

"Oh," says Sophie. "It's chicken and rice casserole soup. But don't ask for the recipe. It's a secret."

Answer the questions.

1. What is Sophie making a chicken and rice casserole for?

2. What is she looking at while she is cutting up the ingredients?

3. How many ounces are in 1½ quarts of chicken stock?

4. What is overflowing?

5. What does Sophie move everything into?

6. How does this chicken and rice casserole look?

7. How many ounces are in 1½ cups of chicken stock?

8. How does the casserole look and smell after she stirs it for a while?

9. What does Sophie bring to the party?

10. What does Sophie say about the recipe?

Complete the sentences.

| ingredients | ounces | soup | recipe |
| quarts | casserole | pot | cups |

1. Sophie is making a chicken and rice _____.

2. Sophie is looking at the recipe while she is cutting up the _____.

3. She reads, "Add 1½ _____ of chicken stock."

4. Sophie converts that to 48 _____. That's a lot of liquid!

5. She needs to move everything into a big _____.

6. Sophie looks at the _____ again. Sophie is wrong.

7. It says, "Add 1½ _____ of chicken stock." That's only 12 ounces.

8. Sophie was looking at a recipe for chicken and rice _____!

Matching: Definitions

_____ 1. convert   a. to find out the size, amount, or weight of something

_____ 2. smell   b. to go over the top of the container

_____ 3. pour   c. to move a spoon through a liquid

_____ 4. measure   d. to change one measuring unit to another

_____ 5. stir   e. to have a particular odor

_____ 6. overflow   f. to let liquid flow from a container

Talking to Sophie's Sister

Practice the dialog with a partner.

A. Yum. What is this?

B. It's chicken and rice casserole soup.

A. I thought you were making a chicken and rice casserole.

B. Yes. But I changed my mind.

A. It's delicious. Can I have the recipe?

B. Sorry. It's a secret.

Liquid Measures

Look at the table Sophie uses to convert cups to ounces. Then answer the questions.

1 cup = 8 fluid ounces = ½ pint = 237 milliliters
2 cups = 16 fluid ounces = 1 pint = 474 milliliters
4 cups = 32 fluid ounces = 1 quart = 946 milliliters
4 quarts = 128 fluid ounces = 1 gallon = 3.784 liters

1. How many liquid ounces are in 1 cup? _____

2. How many cups are in 1 pint? _____

3. How many milliliters are in 1 pint? _____

4. How many quarts are in 4 cups? _____

5. How many fluid ounces are in 1 gallon? _____

6. How many liters are in 4 quarts or 1 gallon? _____

Listening

Listen. Write the numbers you hear. The first one is done for you.

1. Add ____1½____ cups of chicken stock.

2. Put in _____ ounces of low-fat milk.

3. Use _____ cup of honey.

4. Stir in _____ ounces of tomato juice.

5. This recipe calls for _____ ounces of fish stock.

6. Add _____ cup of water to the soup.

7. Put in _____ cup of apple juice.

8. You will need _____ cups of lemon juice.

Pronunciation and Writing

Say the words from the story. Write the number of syllables in each word. Underline the stressed syllable.

1. ingredients ____   6. casserole ____   11. delicious ____

2. liquid ____   7. chicken ____   12. evening ____

3. ounces ____   8. overflowing ____   13. cookbook ____

4. everything ____   9. party ____   14. converts ____

5. measures ____   10. recipe ____   15. actually ____

What about you?

Circle *Yes* or *No.* Then write questions and ask your partner.

Yes   No   1. I sometimes make a chicken and rice casserole.

<u>Do you sometimes make a chicken and rice casserole?</u>

Yes   No   2. I look at recipes while I cook.

_____

Yes   No   3. I always measure ingredients.

_____

Yes   No   4. I sometimes convert cups to ounces or milliliters.

_____

Yes   No   5. I have a recipe that is a secret.

_____

Topics for Discussion or Writing

1. Do you sometimes make food for a party? If so, what do you like to make?

2. Do you have a cookbook at home? If so, what kind of recipes does it have?

3. What things help you measure ingredients in your kitchen?

Lesson 5

Reading Glasses

Viktor is having vision problems. Lately, it's very difficult to read. Viktor can't fill out forms. He can't read books and magazines. He can't read numbers in the telephone book. The print is too small. Viktor asks his wife, Anya, to help him.

One day, Anya says, "Viktor, please see an optometrist. You need to have an eye exam. You probably need reading glasses." So Viktor and Anya go to the optometrist's office.

The receptionist asks Viktor to fill out a form. "I can't read this," says Viktor. "Can you please help me?" Anya helps Viktor fill out the form. Then Anya picks up a magazine. She reads an article and laughs. "What's so funny?" asks Viktor. So Anya reads the article to Viktor.

Finally, the optometrist examines Viktor. His eyes are okay, but he needs reading glasses. "These will help you a lot," says the optometrist.

At home, Viktor tries out his new reading glasses. He picks up the newspaper. He can read it very well. Viktor and Anya are very happy. In the evening, they decide to go out for dinner. "Will you please call and make a reservation?" asks Anya. "The number for the restaurant is in the telephone book."

"Sure," says Viktor. "But first, can you please help me find my reading glasses?"

Answer the questions.

1. What kind of problems is Viktor having?

2. What is it very difficult to do lately?

3. What can't Viktor fill out?

4. Why can't he read numbers in the telephone book?

5. Who does Anya want Viktor to see?

6. Who helps Viktor fill out the form?

7. What does Anya read to Viktor?

8. What kind of glasses does Viktor need?

9. Where do Viktor and Anya decide to go in the evening?

10. Where is the number for the restaurant?

Complete the sentences.

optometrist	newspaper	exam	forms
wife	glasses	magazines	numbers

1. Viktor can't fill out _____.

2. He can't read books and _____.

3. He can't read _____ in the telephone book.

4. Viktor asks his _____, Anya, to help him.

5. One day, Anya says, "Viktor, please see an _____."

6. Viktor goes to the optometrist's office and has an eye _____.

7. His eyes are okay, but he needs reading _____.

8. Now Viktor can read the _____ very well.

Matching: Definitions

_____ 1. glasses   a. eyesight

_____ 2. optometrist   b. words and numbers on paper

_____ 3. print   c. the short form of *examination;* a test

_____ 4. reservation   d. what you wear over your eyes to see better

_____ 5. vision   e. an arrangement to keep something for you

_____ 6. exam   f. a person who tests your eyes

Talking About a Vision Problem

Practice the dialog with a partner.

A. Can you please help me?

B. Sure. What do you need?

A. I can't read this number. The print is too small.

B. Please see an optometrist. You need to have an
eye exam.

A. Yes, I know. I'll make an appointment.

B. You probably need reading glasses.

Check the good ideas.

You are having vision problems. Lately, it's very difficult to read. Check (✔) the things that are
good to do. Write other ideas on the lines below.

_____ go to an ophthalmologist   _____ go to an optometrist

_____ have an eye exam   _____ stop reading and watch TV instead

_____ buy books with large print   _____ buy inexpensive reading glasses

_____ use a magnifying glass to read   _____ hold books far away from your face

_____ ask someone to read for you   _____ have eye surgery

_____   _____

Listening

Listen. Write the missing word. The first one is done for you.

1. Viktor is having _____vision_____ problems.

2. Viktor _____ fill out forms.

3. He can't _____ books and magazines.

4. He can't read _____ in the telephone book.

5. Finally, the optometrist _____ Viktor.

6. His _____ are okay, but he needs reading glasses.

7. At home, Viktor tries out his new reading _____.

8. Viktor picks up the _____. He can read it very _____.

Pronunciation and Writing

Say the words from the story. Write the number of syllables in each word. Underline the stressed syllable.

1. magazines ____

2. glasses ____

3. optometrist ____

4. examines ____

5. vision ____

6. telephone ____

7. reading ____

8. newspaper ____

9. reservation ____

10. exam ____

11. receptionist ____

12. difficult ____

13. article ____

14. funny ____

15. restaurant ____

What about you?

Circle *Yes* or *No*. Then write questions and ask your partner.

Yes   No   1. I have vision problems.

Do you have vision problems? _____

Yes   No   2. I sometimes see an optometrist or an ophthalmologist.

_____

Yes   No   3. I need glasses.

_____

Yes   No   4. I sometimes need help to fill out forms.

_____

Yes   No   5. I think the print is too small in some books and magazines.

_____

Topics for Discussion or Writing

1. Do you have eye exams? If so, how often do you have them?

2. Do you wear glasses? If so, why do you need them?

3. Is there an optometrist's office in your neighborhood? If so, where is it?

Lesson 6

Expensive Cappuccinos

Fazia is a college student. Every morning, she goes to a coffee house for a large cappuccino. It costs $3.50. That's very expensive for coffee and milk, but Fazia likes it. It also helps her stay awake in class.

One morning, Fazia notices a Help Wanted sign in the coffee house. She asks for an application and fills it out. Then she buys her cappuccino and goes to class.

Later, Susan, the manager of the coffee house, calls Fazia. She wants her to come in for an interview. Fazia arrives on time for the interview the next morning. She shakes hands with Susan. Susan asks her about her work experience. Fazia tells Susan about her past jobs and gives her three references.

Susan likes Fazia and hires her. Fazia will work mornings, Monday through Friday, from 6:00 to 9:30. That's a good schedule because her first class begins at 10:00. Fazia understands that the job only pays minimum wage. But free cappuccinos will save her $17.50 a week.

Fazia starts work the next morning. She learns to make many different coffee drinks. At 9:30, Fazia gets ready to leave.

"Thanks," says Susan. "See you tomorrow."

"Oh," says Fazia. "Before I leave, I'd like a large cappuccino."

"Sure," says Susan. "That will be $3.50."

Answer the questions.

1. Where does Fazia go every morning?

2. How much does a large cappuccino cost?

3. What does the cappuccino help her do?

4. What does Fazia notice one morning in the coffee house?

5. Who calls Fazia later?

6. What does Susan ask Fazia about at the interview?

7. How many references does Fazia give Susan?

8. When will Fazia work?

9. How much does the job pay?

10. How much will free cappuccinos save Fazia every week?

Complete the sentences.

manager	cappuccinos	application	references
interview	experience	sign	minimum wage

1. Fazia notices a Help Wanted _____ in the coffee house.

2. She asks for an _____ and fills it out.

3. Later, Susan, the _____ of the coffee house, calls Fazia.

4. Fazia arrives on time for the _____ the next morning.

5. Susan asks her about her work _____.

6. Fazia tells Susan about her past jobs and gives her three _____.

7. Fazia understands that the job only pays _____.

8. But free _____ will save her $17.50 a week.

Matching: Definitions

_____ 1. schedule   a. a drink with coffee and milk

_____ 2. hire   b. the days and times you work

_____ 3. references   c. the money you earn for work

_____ 4. awake   d. people who can give information about you

_____ 5. cappuccino   e. not sleeping

_____ 6. wage   f. to give someone a job

An Interview with the Manager

Practice the dialog with a partner.

A. Can you tell me about your work experience?

B. Yes. Last summer, I worked at Max's Bakery.

A. Do you have any references?

B. Yes. I have three. I wrote them on this paper.

A. Are you available in the early morning?

B. Yes. That's perfect. My first class begins at 10:00.

Check the good ideas.

You have a job interview. Check (✔) the things that are good to do. Write other ideas on the lines below.

_____ arrive on time

_____ drink a large cappuccino

_____ shake hands with the manager

_____ ask about wages

_____ ask about vacation

_____ ask for more than minimum wage

_____ talk about days and times you can work

_____ answer questions about your work experience

_____ ask about free things you can have

_____ give the manager some references

_____   _____

Listening

Listen. Write the prices you hear. The first one is done for you.

1. A large cappuccino will be $__3.50__.

2. Your medium iced tea is $_____.

3. A small espresso is $_____.

4. The medium coffee is $_____.

5. That will be $_____ for the small caffe latte.

6. A large hot chocolate is $_____.

7. The small bottled water is $_____.

8. A large iced mocha is $_____.

Pronunciation and Writing

Say the words from the story. Write the number of syllables in each word. Underline the stressed syllable.

1. interview ____   6. morning ____   11. understands ____

2. schedule ____   7. application ____   12. experience ____

3. minimum ____   8. cappuccino ____   13. awake ____

4. college ____   9. different ____   14. references ____

5. manager ____   10. tomorrow ____   15. coffee ____

What about you?

Circle *Yes* or *No*. Then write questions and ask your partner.

Yes **No** 1. I drink coffee every morning.

Do you drink coffee every morning?

Yes **No** 2. I go to a coffee house every morning.

_____

Yes **No** 3. I sometimes fill out job applications.

_____

Yes **No** 4. I always arrive on time for job interviews.

_____

Yes **No** 5. I have references.

_____

Topics for Discussion or Writing

1. Do you sometimes buy a special drink? If so, what is it? How much do you spend a week on these drinks?

2. Do you have a job? If so, what is your schedule at work?

3. What is a good way to find a job if you are looking for one?

Lesson 7

Buying Generic

Ruben goes shopping for his family every week. He likes to do the shopping. Ruben thinks he spends less money than his wife, Alicia. For one thing, Ruben always buys some generic items at the supermarket. Ruben thinks generic items are the same as name brands, but much cheaper.

Sometimes Alicia complains about the generic items. She says, "The generic item is not always the same." For example, she doesn't like the generic dishwashing soap. Alicia says, "I need to use a lot more when I wash the dishes. So it isn't cheaper."

One day, Alicia is looking in a drawer. She finds a coupon for *Happy Dishes* dishwashing soap. She hands the coupon to Ruben. "Please buy this brand of dishwashing soap the next time you go shopping. If you use the coupon, *Happy Dishes* dishwashing soap is the same price as the generic one."

On Saturday, Ruben goes shopping. At the supermarket, he finds generic paper towels, cereal, butter, rice, and shampoo. He also finds *Happy Dishes* dishwashing soap. He puts it into his shopping cart. Then he goes to the cashier.

"*Happy Dishes* dishwashing soap is three dollars!" says Ruben. "I'm glad I have a coupon for seventy-five cents off."

"Sorry," says the cashier. "This coupon expired last week. Try the generic dishwashing soap. It's much cheaper."

Answer the questions.

1. How often does Ruben go shopping for his family?

2. What does he always buy at the supermarket?

3. What does Ruben think about generic items?

4. What generic item doesn't Alicia like?

5. What does Alicia find in a drawer?

6. If you use the coupon, how much is *Happy Dishes*?

7. What generic items does Ruben find on Saturday?

8. How much is *Happy Dishes* dishwashing soap?

9. How many cents off is the coupon for?

10. When did the coupon expire?

Complete the sentences.

puts	thinks	goes	buys
complains	finds	doesn't like	says

1. Ruben always _____ generic items at the supermarket.

2. He _____ generic items are the same as name brands, but much cheaper.

3. Sometimes Alicia _____ about the generic items.

4. She _____ the generic dishwashing soap.

5. She _____ a coupon for *Happy Dishes* dishwashing soap.

6. On Saturday, Ruben _____ shopping.

7. He _____ *Happy Dishes* dishwashing soap into his shopping cart.

8. "Sorry," _____ the cashier. "This coupon expired last week."

Matching: Definitions

_____ 1. name brand   a. a store product with a plain label

_____ 2. coupon   b. the liquid you use to wash dishes

_____ 3. dishwashing soap   c. a paper that can give you a discount

_____ 4. price   d. a person who takes money from customers

_____ 5. cashier   e. the cost of something

_____ 6. generic item   f. a product from a large company with a noticeable label

Talking to the Cashier

Practice the dialog with a partner.

A. I have a coupon for that dishwashing soap.

B. Okay. Thanks.

A. It's for seventy-five cents off.

B. Sorry, but this coupon expired last week.

A. Really? Well, I don't want to pay three dollars for this name brand.

B. Try the generic dishwashing soap. It's much cheaper.

Check the good ideas.

You want to spend less money when you go shopping. Check (✔) the things that are good to do. Write other ideas on the lines below.

_____ always buy generic items   _____ buy items on sale

_____ use coupons   _____ buy in large quantities

_____ shop at small grocery stores   _____ shop at large club stores

_____ always buy name brands   _____ use expired coupons

_____ look at supermarket ads   _____ compare prices of different brands

_____   _____

Listening

Listen. Write the missing word.

1. Ruben goes _____ for his family every week.

2. Ruben thinks he spends less _____ than his wife, Alicia.

3. For one thing, Ruben always buys _____ items at the supermarket.

4. Ruben thinks generic items are the same as name brands, but much _____.

5. Alicia finds a _____ for *Happy Dishes* dishwashing soap.

6. With the coupon, *Happy Dishes* is the same _____ as the generic soap.

7. He puts it into his shopping cart. Then he goes to the _____.

8. "Sorry," says the cashier. "This coupon _____ last week."

Pronunciation and Writing

Say the words from the story. Write the number of syllables in each word. Underline the stressed syllable.

1. supermarket ____

2. complains ____

3. cereal ____

4. expired ____

5. shampoo ____

6. coupon ____

7. items ____

8. generic ____

9. family ____

10. cheaper ____

11. cashier ____

12. dishwashing ____

What about you?

Circle *Yes* or *No.* Then write questions and ask your partner.

Yes   No   1. I go shopping for my family every week.

Do you go shopping for your family every week?

Yes   No   2. I always buy generic items at the supermarket.

_____

Yes   No   3. I think generic items are the same as name brands.

_____

Yes   No   4. I use coupons when I go shopping.

_____

Yes   No   5. I check to see if my coupons are expired.

_____

Topics for Discussion or Writing

1. Do you buy any generic items? If so, what generic items do you buy?

2. Do you buy any name brand items? If so, what name brand items do you buy?

3. Where can you find coupons to use at a supermarket?

Lesson 8

Looking for ATMs

Tonight Soren is out with his sister, Mina. He is taking her to dinner and a movie for her birthday. Soren doesn't have a lot of money with him. He needs to withdraw some cash at an ATM (Automatic Teller Machine).

Soren and Mina walk to the ATM on First Avenue. Soren inserts his card and enters his PIN (Personal Identification Number). On the screen, Soren reads that there is a $3 service charge for this ATM. He doesn't want to pay a $3 service charge. Soren cancels his transaction.

Soren and Mina walk to another ATM outside a bank on Third Avenue. This is a branch of Soren's bank, so there is no service charge for the ATM. But there is a problem. A sign on this ATM says, "Temporarily Out of Service."

Soren knows there is another ATM on Fifth Avenue. Mina sighs, but Soren promises it will take just a minute. They walk to that ATM, but there is a long line of people waiting to use it. It's also getting very cold outside.

"Forget it!" says Mina. "I can lend you the money. I don't want to look for any more ATMs. It's my birthday. Let's go to dinner!"

"Thanks," says Soren. "I'll pay you back tomorrow."

"Okay," says Mina. "But there's a $5 service charge."

Answer the questions.

1. Who is Soren out with tonight?

2. Where is he taking her for her birthday?

3. What does he need to do at an ATM?

4. What does he enter after he inserts his card?

5. How much is the service charge at this ATM?

6. What does Soren do with his transaction?

7. What does the sign say on the ATM on Third Avenue?

8. What is the problem with another ATM on Fifth Avenue?

9. What does Mina say she can lend Soren?

10. When can Soren pay her back?

Complete the sentences.

birthday	transaction	money	PIN
ATM	sign	line	service charge

1. Soren needs to withdraw some cash at an _____.

2. Soren inserts his card and enters his _____.

3. Soren reads that there is a $3 _____ for this ATM.

4. Soren cancels his _____.

5. At the next ATM, a _____ says, "Temporarily Out of Service."

6. They walk to another ATM, but there is a long _____ of people.

7. "Forget it!" says Mina. "I can lend you the _____."

8. Then she says, "It's my _____. Let's go to dinner!"

Matching: Definitions

_____ 1. lend

_____ 2. withdraw

_____ 3. sigh

_____ 4. insert

_____ 5. pay back

_____ 6. cancel

a. to breathe out loudly and slowly

b. to return money

c. to stop something from happening

d. to take out

e. to put something in

f. to let someone have something for a short time

Talking About the ATM

Practice the dialog with a partner.

A. This will take just a minute. Then we can go to dinner.

B. But look at this long line of people waiting to use the ATM!

A. Brrr. And it's getting cold outside.

B. Forget it! I can lend you the money.

A. Thanks. I'll pay you back tomorrow.

B. Don't forget my $5 service charge.

Matching

Match the words and pictures. Write the words on the lines below.

get cash	insert your card	enter your PIN

1. _____ 2. _____ 3. _____

Listening

Listen. Check (✔) the correct sentence.

1. _____ a. He needs to withdraw some cash.

   _____ b. He needs to deposit some cash.

2. _____ a. He takes out his card.

   _____ b. He puts in his card.

3. _____ a. It costs $3 to use this ATM.

   _____ b. He needs to put $3 in the ATM.

4. _____ a. He gets cash from the ATM.

   _____ b. He stops using the ATM.

5. _____ a. Soren can use this ATM.

   _____ b. This ATM isn't working.

6. _____ a. Soren will need to wait a long time.

   _____ b. Soren can get cash right away.

7. _____ a. Soren can lend his sister money.

   _____ b. Soren can borrow the money.

8. _____ a. Soren will walk to another ATM.

   _____ b. Soren will return the money soon.

Pronunciation and Writing

Say the words from the story. Write the number of syllables in each word. Underline the stressed syllable.

1. withdraw _____

2. service _____

3. transaction _____

4. machine _____

5. teller _____

6. automatic _____

7. money _____

8. birthday _____

9. identification _____

10. temporarily _____

11. inserts _____

12. personal _____

13. number _____

14. tomorrow _____

15. cancels _____

What about you?

Circle *Yes* or *No*. Then write questions and ask your partner.

Yes   No   1. I sometimes take someone to dinner and a movie.

Do you sometimes take someone to dinner and a movie?

Yes   No   2. I sometimes need to withdraw cash.

_____

Yes   No   3. I sometimes go to an ATM.

_____

Yes   No   4. I pay a service charge when I use an ATM.

_____

Yes   No   5. I sometimes see a long line of people waiting to use an ATM.

_____

Topics for Discussion or Writing

1. Do you like to go out on your birthday? If so, what do you like to do?

2. Do you sometimes go to an ATM? If so, where is it?

3. What transactions can you do at an ATM?

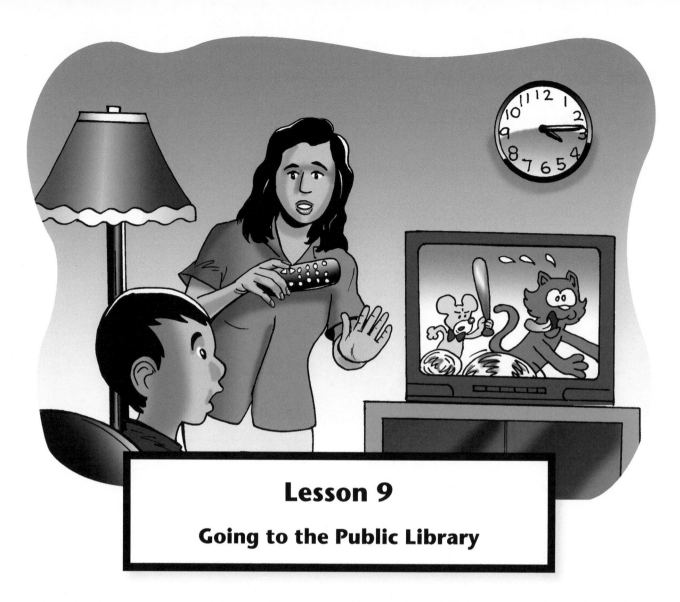

Lesson 9

Going to the Public Library

Marina's seven-year-old son, Dario, watches a lot of TV. He watches TV in the morning before school. He watches TV in the afternoon after school. He watches more TV in the evening after dinner. Dario probably watches four hours of TV every day. Marina knows it's too much. It isn't good for Dario to watch so much TV. It's a bad habit. Finally, Marina decides to do something about it.

In the middle of his afternoon cartoons, Marina turns off the TV. "Why did you do that?" asks Dario.

"Let's do something different today," says Marina. "We can go to the public library. There is a wonderful world outside of the TV, Dario. You need to start reading more."

Marina and Dario arrive at the public library. They walk inside and go to the children's section. Marina feels excited. She looks through the shelves and chooses some books to take home. She picks up some picture books. She picks up two chapter books that Dario can read. Dario is happy, too. He picks up a book about animals and a book about sports. Then, suddenly, Dario runs to another shelf in the children's section.

"Do you see something interesting?" asks Marina.

"Yes!" says Dario. "Can you believe this, Mom? They have videos and DVDs!"

Answer the questions.

1. How old is Marina's son, Dario?

2. When does Dario watch TV?

3. How many hours of TV does Dario probably watch every day?

4. What does Marina do in the middle of his afternoon cartoons?

5. Where does Marina say they can go?

6. Which section do they go to at the public library?

7. How does Marina feel?

8. What books does she pick up for Dario?

9. What books does Dario pick up?

10. What is on another shelf in the children's section?

Complete the sentences.

decides	runs	picks up	says
looks through	isn't	turns off	watches

1. Dario probably _____ four hours of TV every day.

2. It _____ good for Dario to watch so much TV.

3. Marina _____ to do something about it.

4. In the middle of his afternoon cartoons, Marina _____ the TV.

5. Marina _____, "We can go to the public library."

6. She _____ the shelves and chooses some books to take home.

7. Dario _____ a book about animals and a book about sports.

8. Then he _____ to another shelf in the children's section. It has videos and DVDs.

Matching: Definitions

_____ 1. shelves   a. programs with characters that are drawn, not real

_____ 2. chapter books   b. a special area

_____ 3. cartoons   c. movies or other programs recorded on videotape

_____ 4. section   d. a place where you can read or borrow books

_____ 5. videos   e. books divided into different parts

_____ 6. public library   f. flat surfaces where you put things

Talking to the Librarian

Practice the dialog with a partner.

A. I'd like to check out these books, please.

B. Sure. May I see your library card?

A. Yes. Here it is.

B. Thank you. These books are due in three weeks.

A. Is there a fine if we return them late?

B. Yes. The fine is ten cents a day per book.

Check the good ideas.

Your child watches too much TV. Check (✔) the things that are good to do. Write other ideas on the lines below.

_____ turn off the TV   _____ allow only thirty minutes of TV a day

_____ go to the public library   _____ get angry and unplug the TV

_____ tell your child to play outside   _____ buy some books to read at home

_____ break the TV   _____ help your child develop good habits

_____ get some videos and DVDs   _____ start reading more with your child

_____   _____

Listening

Listen. Write the missing word.

1. Marina and Dario arrive at the public _____.

2. They walk inside and go to the children's _____.

3. Marina looks through the shelves and chooses some _____ to take home.

4. She picks up some _____ books.

5. She picks up two _____ books that Dario can read.

6. Dario picks up a book about _____ and a book about sports.

7. Then, suddenly, Dario runs to another shelf in the _____ section.

8. Dario says, "Can you believe this, Mom? They have _____ and DVDs!"

Pronunciation and Writing

Say the words from the story. Write the number of syllables in each word. Underline the stressed syllable.

1. cartoons _____

2. wonderful _____

3. chooses _____

4. habit _____

5. reading _____

6. library _____

7. animals _____

8. chapter _____

9. videos _____

10. picture _____

11. children's _____

12. public _____

56   Lesson 9 Going to the Public Library

What about you?

Circle *Yes* or *No*. Then write questions and ask your partner.

Yes   No   1. I watch a lot of TV.

Do you watch a lot of TV? _____

Yes   No   2. I think watching a lot of TV is a bad habit.

_____

Yes   No   3. I watch TV in the evening after dinner.

_____

Yes   No   4. I sometimes go to the public library.

_____

Yes   No   5. I need to start reading more.

_____

Topics for Discussion or Writing

1. Do you watch TV? If so, what kinds of programs do you like to watch?

2. Do you read books? If so, what kinds of books do you like to read?

3. What kinds of habits do you think are bad?

Lesson 10

Apartment Problems

Hakim is looking for a new apartment. He sees a For Rent sign in front of a building in a nice neighborhood. Hakim walks inside and finds the manager. "Can I see the apartment for rent?" asks Hakim.

"Of course," says the manager. "The apartment is in excellent condition."

Hakim walks into the apartment. The walls are very dirty. "No problem," says the manager. "You just need a painter." In the kitchen, the sink is clogged and the faucet is dripping. "No problem," says the manager. "You just need a plumber. I know someone. She isn't very expensive." In the bedroom, the electricity doesn't work. "No problem," says the manager. "You just need an electrician. He can fix that." Then Hakim notices cockroaches crawling across the floor. "No problem," says the manager. "You just need an exterminator." Hakim points to a broken window. "No problem. You just need a handyman," says the manager. "That's easy to repair."

The manager has a rental agreement in his hand. He wants to rent this apartment to Hakim. "When do you want to move in?" asks the manager.

"Sorry," says Hakim. "I don't want to pay for a painter, a plumber, an electrician, an exterminator, and a handyman. Those are your problems. You just need another tenant."

Answer the questions.

1. What is Hakim looking for?

2. Where does he see a For Rent sign?

3. Who does Hakim find inside?

4. How are the walls in the apartment?

5. What is the problem in the kitchen?

6. What doesn't work in the bedroom?

7. What does Hakim notice crawling across the floor?

8. What does the manager say is easy to repair?

9. What does the manager have in his hand?

10. Who doesn't Hakim want to pay for?

Complete the sentences.

electricity	problems	faucet	agreement
apartment	walls	window	cockroaches

1. "Can I see the _____ for rent?" asks Hakim.

2. Hakim walks into the apartment. The _____ are very dirty.

3. The kitchen sink is clogged, and the _____ is dripping.

4. In the bedroom, the _____ doesn't work.

5. Then Hakim notices _____ crawling across the floor.

6. Hakim points to a broken _____.

7. The manager has a rental _____ in his hand.

8. Hakim says, "Those are your _____."

Matching: Definitions

_____ 1. plumber   a. a person who rents an apartment

_____ 2. handyman   b. a person who kills insects and small animals

_____ 3. painter   c. a person who fixes electrical equipment

_____ 4. tenant   d. a person who repairs many different things

_____ 5. exterminator   e. a person who paints

_____ 6. electrician   f. a person who fixes pipes, sinks, toilets, etc.

Talking to an Apartment Manager

Practice the dialog with a partner.

A. Can I see the apartment for rent?

B. Sure. I can show it to you right now.

A. Is this a safe area?

B. Yes. This is a very nice neighborhood.

A. I don't want a place with a lot of problems.

B. Don't worry. The apartment is in excellent condition.

Apartment Problems

What does the manager say about each problem? Read the example. Then write new sentences.

Problem	The manager says:
1. The walls are very dirty.	<u>No problem. You just need a painter.</u>
2. The sink is clogged, and the faucet is dripping.	_____
3. The electricity doesn't work.	_____
4. There are cockroaches crawling across the floor.	_____
5. There is a broken window.	_____

Listening

Listen. Check (✔) the correct sentence.

1. _____ a. He needs the tenant.
   _____ b. He needs the manager.

2. _____ a. He needs a painter.
   _____ b. He needs an electrician.

3. _____ a. He needs a plumber.
   _____ b. He needs an exterminator.

4. _____ a. He needs a handyman.
   _____ b. He needs an electrician.

5. _____ a. He needs an exterminator.
   _____ b. He needs a plumber.

6. _____ a. He needs a painter.
   _____ b. He needs a handyman.

7. _____ a. He wants to rent this apartment.
   _____ b. He wants to repair this apartment.

8. _____ a. He wants to move in.
   _____ b. He doesn't want to move in.

Pronunciation and Writing

Say the words from the story. Write the number of syllables in each word. Underline the stressed syllable.

1. apartment _____

2. plumber _____

3. neighborhood _____

4. handyman _____

5. exterminator _____

6. tenant _____

7. electricity _____

8. manager _____

9. repair _____

10. painter _____

11. condition _____

12. electrician _____

13. agreement _____

14. dripping _____

15. cockroaches _____

What about you?

Circle *Yes* or *No*. Then write questions and ask your partner.

Yes   No   1. I need a painter.

Do you need a painter? _____

Yes   No   2. I need a plumber.

_____

Yes   No   3. I need an electrician.

_____

Yes   No   4. I need an exterminator.

_____

Yes   No   5. I need a handyman.

_____

Topics for Discussion or Writing

1. What kinds of problems do you have in your home? How can you fix them?

2. Who can you call when you have problems at home?

3. What other problems can a handyman help you with? How can you find a handyman?

Lesson 11

Things in the Mail

Katya opens her mailbox every afternoon. At 86 years old, Katya really enjoys getting mail. She doesn't receive a lot of phone calls and visitors. Katya keeps in touch with people through cards and letters.

Today there are several things in the mail. Katya opens a pink envelope. It is from Robert and Deborah Miller. They lived in her building a few years ago. It is a birth announcement for their new baby girl, Isabelle. Katya feels very happy for them. "How nice," thinks Katya. "I need to buy a baby gift and send it to them."

Katya opens another envelope. It is a high school graduation announcement from her friend's grandson, Tony. "Oh," thinks Katya. "Well, I don't know Tony very well. But I think I need to send him a card and some money."

Katya picks up another envelope. This one is from her great-niece, Amanda. She is trying to raise money for a school trip. There is a donation form enclosed and a short note from Amanda. It says, "Hi, Auntie! I hope you can make a donation!"

Then Katya finds bills from her doctor and the gas and electric company. Katya sighs. She puts the mail down. "The mail is a little expensive today," she thinks. "I can open the rest of it tomorrow."

Answer the questions.

1. How old is Katya?

2. What does she enjoy getting?

3. How does Katya keep in touch with people?

4. What is in the pink envelope from Robert and Deborah Miller?

5. What does Katya think she needs to do?

6. Who is the high school graduation announcement from?

7. What does Katya think she needs to send Tony?

8. What is her great-niece, Amanda, trying to do?

9. What kind of form is enclosed?

10. What bills does Katya find in the mail?

What is the category?

letters	phone calls	cable company	graduation announcement
phone company	visitors	bills	gas and electric company
donation form	cards	doctor's office	birth announcement

Ways to Keep in Touch	Things in Katya's Mail	Places that Send Bills
1. _____	1. _____	1. _____
2. _____	2. _____	2. _____
3. _____	3. _____	3. _____
4. _____	4. _____	4. _____

Matching: Definitions

_____ 1. birth   a. the daughter of your niece or nephew

_____ 2. envelope   b. a ceremony for students finishing their studies

_____ 3. great-niece   c. a paper cover you put a letter or other mail in

_____ 4. donation   d. a paper that gives news about something

_____ 5. announcement   e. the time when a baby is born

_____ 6. graduation   f. money you give to help an organization

Talking to the Mail Carrier

Practice the dialog with a partner.

A. Do you have any mail for me today?

B. Yes. I have a lot of mail for you.

A. I hope it's not a lot of bills.

B. Sorry, but I think there are a couple of bills in there.

A. Oh, well. I don't have to open them today.

B. Of course not. Enjoy your cards and letters.

Check the good ideas.

Katya needs to send gifts, make a donation, and pay her bills. She doesn't have a lot of money. Check (✔) the things that are good to do. Write other ideas on the lines below.

_____ pay all the bills first

_____ send inexpensive gifts

_____ knit something for the baby

_____ make a very large donation

_____ send cards and no gifts

_____ pay the bills next month

_____ put the donation form in the trash

_____ send $100 to the high school graduate

_____ pay some bills, but not others

_____ tell her great-niece to get a job

_____   _____

Listening

Listen. Write the missing word.

1. Katya keeps in touch with people through cards and _____.

2. Today there are several things in the _____.

3. Katya opens a pink _____ from Robert and Deborah Miller.

4. It is a _____ announcement for their new baby girl, Isabelle.

5. Then there is a high school graduation _____ from her friend's grandson.

6. Her great-niece is trying to raise _____ for a school trip.

7. There is a _____ form enclosed and a short note from Amanda.

8. Katya also finds _____ from her doctor and the gas and electric company.

Pronunciation and Writing

Say the words from the story. Write the number of syllables in each word. Underline the stressed syllable.

1. company ____

2. several ____

3. enclosed ____

4. visitors ____

5. grandson ____

6. graduation ____

7. baby ____

8. announcement ____

9. envelope ____

10. donation ____

11. letters ____

12. mailbox ____

What about you?

Circle *Yes* or *No.* Then write questions and ask your partner.

Yes No   1. I receive a lot of phone calls and visitors.

Do you receive a lot of phone calls and visitors? _____

Yes No   2. I keep in touch with people through cards and letters.

_____

Yes No   3. I sometimes receive birth announcements.

_____

Yes No   4. I sometimes receive graduation announcements.

_____

Yes No   5. I sometimes receive donation forms.

_____

Topics for Discussion or Writing

1. Do you enjoy getting mail? If so, what kind of mail do you enjoy getting?

2. Do you buy a baby gift when someone has a new baby? If so, what kind of gift do you buy?

3. What do you do when someone asks you for a donation? What do you think is a good thing to say when you can't give money?

Lesson 12

A Japanese Tutor

Giselle is a junior in high school. She is taking Japanese for her two-year language requirement. Giselle is usually a very good student, but Japanese is difficult for her. After her third semester, Giselle is not doing well. "Japanese is so hard!" says Giselle. "I want to drop the class!" Luc, her father, is worried about Giselle's grade. He talks with her Japanese teacher and her high school counselor. They both want Giselle to stay in the class. But they recommend getting a tutor for Giselle. After a few phone calls, Luc finds Mr. Sato, an experienced Japanese tutor.

Luc hires Mr. Sato to help Giselle during her fourth semester. Mr. Sato comes to their home two evenings a week. He reviews Giselle's classwork and checks her homework. They do exercises to help Giselle understand, speak, read, and write Japanese. After Mr. Sato comes, everything is clearer for Giselle.

Giselle has an A in Japanese on her final report card. Giselle, her father, the teacher, the counselor, and Mr. Sato are all very happy.

"Congratulations!" says her father. "You finished your language requirement. You don't have to take Japanese anymore."

"I know, Dad," says Giselle. "But I don't want to forget everything! I love Japanese. I want to take it again next year."

Answer the questions.

1. What language is Giselle taking for her two-year language requirement?

2. How is she doing after her third semester?

3. What does Giselle want to do?

4. Who does her father, Luc, talk with?

5. What do Giselle's teacher and counselor recommend?

6. Who does Luc find after a few phone calls?

7. How often does Mr. Sato come to their home?

8. What does Mr. Sato review and check?

9. What grade does Giselle have in Japanese on her final report card?

10. When does she want to take Japanese again?

What is the category?

language	teacher	read	history
understand	speak	science	write
parent	mathematics	tutor	counselor

People Who Help Students	What Giselle Needs to Do	High School Requirements
1. _____	1. _____	1. _____
2. _____	2. _____	2. _____
3. _____	3. _____	3. _____
4. _____	4. _____	4. _____

Matching: Definitions

_____ 1. junior   a. a person who gives advice

_____ 2. grade   b. an eleventh-grade student

_____ 3. tutor   c. something that you have to do

_____ 4. semester   d. a teacher who can help students individually

_____ 5. counselor   e. one half of a school year

_____ 6. requirement   f. a mark for schoolwork, such as *A, B, C, D,* and *F*

Talking to the High School Counselor

Practice the dialog with a partner.

A. My daughter wants to drop her Japanese class.

B. After three semesters, I don't think it's a good idea.

A. But I'm worried about her grade.

B. I understand. But I have a better idea.

A. What do you recommend?

B. I recommend getting your daughter a tutor.

Mr. Sato's Business Card

Read Mr. Sato's business card and answer the questions.

Kenji Sato
Japanese Language Tutor
Certified Instructor

Private tutoring for high school
and college students

Over 12 years of experience

$25 per hour   Excellent references
Phone: (415) 555-9176   E-mail: kenjisato@earthnet.com

---

1. What is Mr. Sato's first name?

2. How many years of experience does he have?

3. How much does he charge?

4. What is his area code? What is his phone number?

5. What is his e-mail address?

Listening

Listen. Check (✔) the correct sentence.

1. _____ a. She is a tenth-grade student.

   _____ b. She is an eleventh-grade student.

2. _____ a. She can understand Japanese.

   _____ b. Japanese is hard for her.

3. _____ a. She wants to stop taking it.

   _____ b. She wants to take it next year.

4. _____ a. She is not doing well.

   _____ b. She has an A.

5. _____ a. Mr. Sato can teach Japanese.

   _____ b. Mr. Sato studies Japanese, too.

6. _____ a. Mr. Sato does Giselle's homework.

   _____ b. Giselle understands Japanese more.

7. _____ a. Everyone is happy.

   _____ b. Everyone is worried.

8. _____ a. She needs one more semester.

   _____ b. She doesn't have to take Japanese.

Pronunciation and Writing

Say the words from the story. Write the number of syllables in each word. Underline the stressed syllable.

1. language _____

2. counselor _____

3. experienced _____

4. reviews _____

5. semester _____

6. junior _____

7. recommend _____

8. report _____

9. understand _____

10. clearer _____

11. Japanese _____

12. requirement _____

13. worried _____

14. tutor _____

15. congratulations _____

What about you?

Circle *Yes* or *No*. Then write questions and ask your partner.

Yes   No   1. I have a two-year language requirement.

<u>Do you have a two-year language requirement?</u>

Yes   No   2. I think English is a difficult language.

_____

Yes   No   3. I sometimes feel worried about grades in school.

_____

Yes   No   4. I do exercises that help me understand, speak, read, and write English.

_____

Yes   No   5. I sometimes get help from an English tutor.

_____

Topics for Discussion or Writing

1. Is there a subject that is very difficult for you? If so, what is it?

2. What is a good way to find a language tutor?

3. What other things can help you learn a language?

Lesson 13

Fishing Regulations

Feng is fishing with his seven-year-old son, Zhu. They are on a pier next to the water. Zhu feels a pull on his fishing line. He reels in a small fish. "Look!" says Zhu. "We have fish for dinner tonight!"

Feng measures the fish with a ruler. It is 8 inches long. Then he checks a paper with the fishing regulations. This fish needs to be at least 12 inches long. "Sorry," says Feng. "We can't keep it."

Zhu is disappointed. He throws the fish back into the water. Feng explains that there are rules about size. They can get a citation if their fish is too small. "We'll have to pay a big fine," says Feng.

A few minutes later, Feng feels a pull on his fishing line. He reels in a different kind of fish. Zhu is excited. He says, "Now we have fish for dinner tonight!"

Feng measures the fish with his ruler. It is 21 inches long. But this fish needs to be at least 24 inches long. Feng throws the fish back into the water.

Feng and Zhu fish all afternoon. But everything they catch is too small. "Oh, well," says Feng. "We don't have fish for dinner tonight."

"That's okay," says Zhu. "Are there regulations about hamburgers?"

Answer the questions.

1. Who is Feng fishing with?

2. Where are they?

3. What does Zhu feel a pull on?

4. What does he reel in?

5. How does Feng measure the fish? Then what does he check?

6. How long is the fish? How long does it need to be?

7. Where does Zhu throw the fish?

8. What can they get if their fish is too small?

9. How long is the next fish? How long does it need to be?

10. How long do Feng and Zhu fish?

Complete the sentences.

regulations	inches	citation	fishing line
dinner	pier	size	fish

1. Feng and Zhu are on a _____ next to the water.

2. Zhu feels a pull on his _____.

3. "Look!" says Zhu. "We have fish for _____ tonight!"

4. Feng measures the fish with a ruler. It is 8 _____ long.

5. Then he checks a paper with the fishing _____.

6. Zhu is disappointed. He throws the _____ back into the water.

7. Feng explains that there are rules about _____.

8. They can get a _____ if their fish is too small.

Matching: Definitions

_____ 1. inches

_____ 2. regulations

_____ 3. ruler

_____ 4. fine

_____ 5. pier

_____ 6. citation

a. a straight stick that can measure things

b. rules or laws about something

c. money you need to pay for breaking a rule

d. a paper that says you did something illegal

e. units equal to 2.54 centimeters

f. a long, flat wooden structure built over water

Talking About Fishing Regulations

Practice the dialog with a partner.

A. Look! We have fish for dinner tonight!

B. Let me measure it. Okay, it's 8 inches long.

A. What do the fishing regulations say?

B. Sorry, but this fish needs to be at least
   12 inches long.

A. Do I have to throw the fish back into the water?

B. Yes. We can get a citation if our fish is too small.

Matching

Match the words and pictures. Write the words on the lines below.

measure the fish	check the regulations	reel in a fish

1. _____

2. _____

3. _____

Listening

Listen. Write the numbers you hear.

1. This fish needs to be at least _____ inches long.

2. Your fish measures _____ inches.

3. This fish is too small. It's only _____ inches.

4. I can keep this fish. It's _____ inches long.

5. Sorry, but this paper says at least _____ inches.

6. That fish is _____ inches long.

7. The regulations say it needs to be _____ inches.

8. His fish is exactly _____ inches long.

Pronunciation and Writing

Say the words from the story. Write the number of syllables in each word. Underline the stressed syllable.

1. fishing _____

2. dinner _____

3. measures _____

4. regulations _____

5. afternoon _____

6. everything _____

7. ruler _____

8. water _____

9. citation _____

10. hamburgers _____

11. tonight _____

12. inches _____

13. excited _____

14. disappointed _____

15. explains _____

What about you?

Circle *Yes* or *No.* Then write questions and ask your partner.

Yes   No   1. I go fishing sometimes.

Do you go fishing sometimes? _____

Yes   No   2. I know where there is a pier next to the water.

_____

Yes   No   3. I like fish for dinner.

_____

Yes   No   4. I know about fishing regulations.

_____

Yes   No   5. I know about fishing citations.

_____

Topics for Discussion or Writing

1. Is there a good place to go fishing in your community? If so, where is it?

2. What kinds of fish do people like to eat for dinner?

3. For what other things can you get a citation?

Lesson 14

A Digital Camera

Delia is 28 years old. Every year, she likes to send her picture to Cindy, her best friend from high school. First, Delia buys a roll of film and inserts it into her camera. Then her mother, Leona, takes twenty-four pictures of Delia. Later, they get the film developed at the photo store. But when Delia looks at the pictures, she is never happy. So Delia buys more film and asks Leona to take more pictures.

This year, Leona has a nice surprise. "Look, Delia," she says. "I have a digital camera." Leona explains that it's better than taking pictures with their old camera. "I can take a lot of pictures of you. We don't need to print the pictures you don't like. We can save time and money."

Delia smiles and poses for the pictures. Leona takes Delia's picture in the living room, dining room, and kitchen. Leona takes about fifty pictures. Then Leona connects her camera to the computer and downloads the pictures. They can see all of the pictures on the screen. Delia looks at them for a long time.

"Okay," says Leona. "Which one do you want to send to Cindy?"

"I don't like any of these," says Delia. "Let's take some more pictures. I look better in the backyard."

Answer the questions.

1. Who does Delia like to send her picture to every year?

2. What does Delia buy and insert into her camera?

3. How many pictures does Delia's mother take of her?

4. Where do they get the film developed later?

5. What nice surprise does Leona have this year?

6. Where does Leona take Delia's picture with the digital camera?

7. How many photos does she take?

8. What does Leona do after she connects her camera to the computer?

9. Where can they see all of the pictures?

10. Where does Delia think she looks better?

Complete the sentences.

explains	has	takes	downloads
buys	likes	poses	looks at

1. Delia _____ to send her picture to Cindy, her best friend from high school.

2. Her mother, Leona, _____ twenty-four pictures of Delia.

3. But when Delia _____ the pictures, she is never happy.

4. So Delia _____ more film and asks Leona to take more pictures.

5. This year, Leona _____ a nice surprise. It's a digital camera.

6. Leona _____ that it's better than taking pictures with their old camera.

7. Delia smiles and _____ for the pictures.

8. Then Leona connects her camera to the computer and _____ the pictures.

Matching: Definitions

_____ 1. picture   a. the thin material you put in cameras to take pictures

_____ 2. screen   b. a photograph

_____ 3. camera   c. the outside area behind your house or apartment

_____ 4. film   d. a device you use to take photos

_____ 5. backyard   e. the flat surface on a computer or TV

Talking About a Digital Camera

Practice the dialog with a partner.

A. I have a new digital camera.

B. Oh, that's nice. Is it better than our old camera?

A. Yes. We don't need to print the pictures you don't like.

B. How can we see the pictures?

A. I connect the camera to the computer and download the pictures.

B. Great. Then we can take a lot of pictures!

Matching

Match the words and pictures. Write the words on the lines below.

download the pictures	take pictures	connect your camera to the computer

1. _____

2. _____

3. _____

Listening

Listen. Write the missing word.

1. Delia likes to send her _____ to Cindy, her best friend from high school.

2. First, Delia buys a roll of _____ and inserts it into her camera.

3. Later, they get the film developed at the _____ store.

4. This year, Leona has a digital _____.

5. They don't need to _____ the pictures Delia doesn't like.

6. Leona takes Delia's picture in the _____ room, dining room, and kitchen.

7. Then Leona connects her camera to the _____ and downloads the pictures.

8. They can see all of the pictures on the _____.

Pronunciation and Writing

Say the words from the story. Write the number of syllables in each word. Underline the stressed syllable.

1. picture _____

2. inserts _____

3. camera _____

4. developed _____

5. surprise _____

6. digital _____

7. poses _____

8. connects _____

9. computer _____

10. downloads _____

11. backyard _____

12. photo _____

What about you?

Circle *Yes* or *No.* Then write questions and ask your partner.

Yes   No   1. I like taking pictures.

<u>*Do you like taking pictures?*</u>

Yes   No   2. I have an old camera.

_____

Yes   No   3. I sometimes get film developed at a photo store.

_____

Yes   No   4. I have a digital camera.

_____

Yes   No   5. I like to send pictures to my family and friends.

_____

Topics for Discussion or Writing

1. Do you have a best friend? If so, how do you know this person?

2. Is there a special place inside or outside your home where you like to take pictures? If so, where is it?

3. Where is a good place in your community to buy a digital camera?

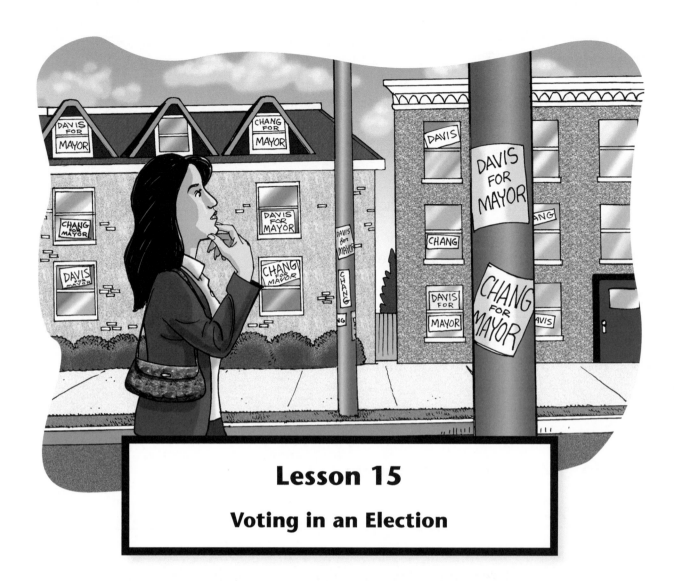

Lesson 15

Voting in an Election

Last year, Fatima became a U.S. citizen. Now she has the right to vote for the first time in the local election. For mayor, Clayton Davis is running against Melissa Chang. Fatima reads about the candidates in her sample ballot. She sees their pictures and reads information about them. She looks at their political parties. She also reads about their plans to help her city. Fatima decides to vote for Melissa Chang.

But Fatima also notices the political advertisements. There are many advertisements for the candidates on TV and on the radio. There are many advertisements in the mail. There are many signs on the street and in apartment windows. Sometimes she gets telephone calls asking her to vote for either Clayton Davis or Melissa Chang.

In the advertisements for Clayton Davis, Melissa Chang seems like the wrong candidate for mayor. In the advertisements for Melissa Chang, Clayton Davis seems like the wrong candidate for mayor. Fatima is confused. Now she doesn't know who to vote for.

Three days before the election, Fatima watches a debate on TV. She listens to the candidates talk for one hour. Fatima understands this more than the advertisements, the signs, and the phone calls. Now she knows who to vote for. Once again, Fatima decides to vote for Melissa Chang.

Answer the questions.

1. When did Fatima become a U.S. citizen?

2. What right does she have for the first time now?

3. Who is Clayton Davis running against for mayor?

4. Where does Fatima read about the candidates?

5. Who does Fatima decide to vote for?

6. Where are there many advertisements for the candidates?

7. How does Melissa Chang seem in the advertisements for Clayton Davis?

8. When does Fatima watch a debate on TV?

9. How long do the candidates talk?

10. Who does Fatima decide to vote for once again?

Complete the sentences.

advertisements	citizen	parties	city
mayor	election	debate	candidates

1. Last year, Fatima became a U.S. _____.

2. Now she has the right to vote for the first time in the local _____.

3. For _____, Clayton Davis is running against Melissa Chang.

4. Fatima reads about the _____ in her sample ballot.

5. She looks at their political _____.

6. She also reads about their plans to help her _____.

7. There are many _____ for the candidates on TV and on the radio.

8. Three days before the election, Fatima watches a _____ on TV.

Matching: Definitions

_____ 1. mayor   a. a person who can legally vote in a country

_____ 2. citizen   b. a person running for public office

_____ 3. election   c. a time when people vote for political leaders

_____ 4. sample ballot   d. information that helps you decide how to vote

_____ 5. debate   e. the elected leader of a city

_____ 6. candidate   f. a public discussion about different topics

Talking About the Election

Practice the dialog with a partner.

A. Who are you going to vote for?

B. I don't know yet. How about you?

A. I like Clayton Davis for mayor.

B. What do you like about him?

A. I like his plans to help our city.

B. Well, I really need to watch the debate on TV.

Check the good ideas.

You have the right to vote for the first time in the local election. Check (✔) the things that are good to do. Write other ideas on the lines below.

_____ read your sample ballot

_____ watch a debate on TV

_____ watch advertisements on TV

_____ listen to telephone calls

_____ read signs on the street

_____ look at the candidates' political parties

_____ vote for your friend's favorite candidate

_____ read advertisements in the mail

_____ listen to advertisements on the radio

_____ read about the candidates' plans

_____   _____

Listening

Listen. Write the missing word.

1. Fatima has the right to vote for the first time in the local _____.

2. For _____, Clayton Davis is running against Melissa Chang.

3. Fatima reads about the candidates in her sample _____.

4. Fatima decides to _____ for Melissa Chang.

5. Fatima also notices the political _____.

6. Fatima is _____. Now she doesn't know who to vote for.

7. Three days before the election, Fatima watches a _____ on TV.

8. She listens to the _____ talk for one hour.

Pronunciation and Writing

Say the words from the story. Write the number of syllables in each word. Underline the stressed syllable.

1. political ____

2. running ____

3. ballot ____

4. information ____

5. parties ____

6. apartment ____

7. citizen ____

8. telephone ____

9. advertisements ____

10. radio ____

11. election ____

12. candidates ____

13. mayor ____

14. confused ____

15. understands ____

What about you?

Circle *Yes* or *No*. Then write questions and ask your partner.

Yes No   1. I vote in elections.

<u>Do you vote in elections?</u>

Yes No   2. I know two candidates who are running against each other.

_____

Yes No   3. I notice political advertisements.

_____

Yes No   4. I like to watch debates on TV.

_____

Yes No   5. I get telephone calls asking me to vote for someone.

_____

Topics for Discussion or Writing

1. Who is the mayor of your city? How does he or she help your city?

2. What are the names of some political parties in the U.S.?

3. What rights does a U.S. citizen have?

Listening Exercise Prompts

Lesson 1, page 8

Listen. Check the correct sentence.

1. This morning, there is a commercial on the radio.
2. Every morning is the same routine.
3. He thinks he needs to change his routine.
4. The bus is crowded.
5. Leftover pizza is not a very good breakfast.
6. It's better to shave after you take a shower.
7. It's better to get dressed after you brush your teeth.
8. "My routine is fine," thinks Bruno.

Lesson 2, page 14

Listen. Check the correct sentence.

1. Tonight there is a big celebration for Edward and Sally.
2. Their children, nieces, nephews, brothers, sisters, and cousins are all there.
3. But there is one person who isn't happy.
4. In her opinion, things aren't quite right.
5. Because the music is rock, Irma says, "Classical is better."
6. They listen to the best wishes of their other guests.
7. Irma also wants to say something. The music stops.
8. "I know," says Irma. "But Howard is better."

Lesson 3, page 20

Listen. Check the correct sentence.

1. Sometimes there is traffic at rush hour.
2. Peter is stuck in a terrible traffic jam.
3. Peter can't go straight.
4. He can't make a U-turn.
5. A man on a motorcycle passes Peter's car.
6. Now Peter is angry.
7. Finally, the police arrive to help clear the traffic jam.
8. Peter is thirty minutes late for work.

Lesson 4, page 26

Listen. Write the numbers you hear. The first one is done for you.

1. Add one and a half cups of chicken stock.
2. Put in sixteen ounces of low-fat milk.
3. Use a quarter cup of honey.
4. Stir in twelve ounces of tomato juice.
5. This recipe calls for thirty-two ounces of fish stock.
6. Add three quarters cup of water to the soup.
7. Put in a half cup of apple juice.
8. You will need one and a quarter cups of lemon juice.

Lesson 5, page 32

Listen. Write the missing word. The first one is done for you.

1. Viktor is having vision problems.
2. Viktor can't fill out forms.
3. He can't read books and magazines.
4. He can't read numbers in the telephone book.
5. Finally, the optometrist examines Viktor.
6. His eyes are okay, but he needs reading glasses.
7. At home, Viktor tries out his new reading glasses.
8. Viktor picks up the newspaper. He can read it very well.

Lesson 6, page 38

Listen. Write the prices you hear. The first one is done for you.

1. A large cappuccino will be three dollars and fifty cents.
2. Your medium iced tea is one dollar and twenty-five cents.
3. A small espresso is one dollar and forty-five cents.
4. The medium coffee is one dollar and seventy cents.
5. That will be two dollars and sixty cents for the small caffe latte.
6. A large hot chocolate is two dollars and seventy cents.

7. The small bottled water is one dollar and forty cents.

8. A large iced mocha is three dollars and seventy-five cents.

Lesson 7, page 44

Listen. Write the missing word.

1. Ruben goes shopping for his family every week.

2. Ruben thinks he spends less money than his wife, Alicia.

3. For one thing, Ruben always buys generic items at the supermarket.

4. Ruben thinks generic items are the same as name brands, but much cheaper.

5. Alicia finds a coupon for *Happy Dishes* dishwashing soap.

6. With the coupon, *Happy Dishes* is the same price as the generic soap.

7. He puts it into his shopping cart. Then he goes to the cashier.

8. "Sorry," says the cashier. "This coupon expired last week."

Lesson 8, page 50

Listen. Check the correct sentence.

1. Soren doesn't have a lot of money with him.

2. Soren inserts his card.

3. Soren reads that there is a $3 service charge for this ATM.

4. Soren cancels his transaction.

5. A sign on this ATM says, "Temporarily Out of Service."

6. There is a long line of people waiting to use the ATM.

7. "Forget it!" says Mina. "I can lend you the money."

8. "Thanks," says Soren. "I'll pay you back tomorrow."

Lesson 9, page 56

Listen. Write the missing word.

1. Marina and Dario arrive at the public library.

2. They walk inside and go to the children's section.

3. Marina looks through the shelves and chooses some books to take home.

4. She picks up some picture books.

5. She picks up two chapter books that Dario can read.

6. Dario picks up a book about animals and a book about sports.

7. Then, suddenly, Dario runs to another shelf in the children's section.

8. Dario says, "Can you believe this, Mom? They have videos and DVDs!"

Lesson 10, page 62

Listen. Check the correct sentence.

1. Hakim wants to see the apartment for rent.

2. The walls are very dirty.

3. In the kitchen, the sink is clogged and the faucet is dripping.

4. In the bedroom, the electricity doesn't work.

5. Hakim notices cockroaches crawling across the floor.

6. Hakim points to a broken window.

7. The manager has a rental agreement in his hand.

8. Hakim says, "Those are your problems. You just need another tenant."

Lesson 11, page 68

Listen. Write the missing word.

1. Katya keeps in touch with people through cards and letters.

2. Today there are several things in the mail.

3. Katya opens a pink envelope from Robert and Deborah Miller.

4. It is a birth announcement for their new baby girl, Isabelle.

5. Then there is a high school graduation announcement from her friend's grandson.

6. Her great-niece is trying to raise money for a school trip.

7. There is a donation form enclosed and a short note from Amanda.

8. Katya also finds bills from her doctor and the gas and electric company.

Lesson 12, page 74

Listen. Check the correct sentence.

1. Giselle is a junior in high school.
2. Japanese is difficult for her.
3. Giselle says, "I want to drop the class!"
4. Luc, her father, is worried about Giselle's grade.
5. After a few phone calls, Luc finds Mr. Sato, an experienced Japanese tutor.
6. After Mr. Sato comes, everything is clearer for Giselle.
7. Giselle has an A in Japanese on her final report card.
8. Giselle's father says, "You finished your language requirement."

Lesson 13, page 80

Listen. Write the numbers you hear.

1. This fish needs to be at least twelve inches long.
2. Your fish measures twenty-six inches.
3. This fish is too small. It's only nine inches.
4. I can keep this fish. It's seventeen inches long.
5. Sorry, but this paper says at least twenty-one inches.
6. That fish is eleven inches long.
7. The regulations say it needs to be twenty-eight inches.
8. His fish is exactly fourteen inches long.

Lesson 14, page 86

Listen. Write the missing word.

1. Delia likes to send her picture to Cindy, her best friend from high school.
2. First, Delia buys a roll of film and inserts it into her camera.
3. Later, they get the film developed at the photo store.
4. This year, Leona has a digital camera.
5. They don't need to print the pictures Delia doesn't like.
6. Leona takes Delia's picture in the living room, dining room, and kitchen.
7. Then Leona connects her camera to the computer and downloads the pictures.
8. They can see all of the pictures on the screen.

Lesson 15, page 92

Listen. Write the missing word.

1. Fatima has the right to vote for the first time in the local election.
2. For mayor, Clayton Davis is running against Melissa Chang.
3. Fatima reads about the candidates in her sample ballot.
4. Fatima decides to vote for Melissa Chang.
5. Fatima also notices the political advertisements.
6. Fatima is confused. Now she doesn't know who to vote for.
7. Three days before the election, Fatima watches a debate on TV.
8. She listens to the candidates talk for one hour.